EYE ON HISTORICAL SOURCES

Questions and Answers About THE ALAMO

DWAYNE HICKS

PowerKiDS press

New York

Published in 2019 by The Rosen Publishing Group, Inc.
29 East 21st Street, New York, NY 10010

First Edition

Editor: Greg Roza
Book Design: Michael Flynn

Photo Credits: Cover Sipley/ClassicStock/Getty Images; cover, pp. 1, 3–32 NuConcept Dezine/Shutterstock.com; p. 5 MPI/Archive Photos/Getty Images; p. 7 courtesy of the Wittliff Collections, Texas State University; p. 9 courtesy of the John Carter Brown Library at Brown University; p. 11 Sean Pavone/Shutterstock.com; p. 12 De Agostini Picture Library/Getty Images; p. 13 Universal Images Group/Getty Images; p. 14 Center for American History, The University of Texas at Austin; p. 15 Corbis Historical/Getty Images; p. 16 Bettmann/Getty Images; p. 17 Western Americana Collection, Beinecke Library, Yale University; pp. 19, 23, 27 Texas State Library & Archives Commission; p. 20 State Preservation Board, Austin, Texas; p. 21 Burstein Collection/Corbis/VCG/Getty Images; p. 25 © North Wind Picture Archives/Alamy; p. 29 © Old Paper Studios/Alamy.

Cataloging-in-Publication Data

Names: Hicks, Dwayne.
Title: Questions and answers about the Alamo / Dwayne Hicks.
Description: New York : PowerKids Press, 2019. | Series: Eye on historical sources | Includes glossary and index.
Identifiers: LCCN ISBN 9781538341087 (pbk.) | ISBN 9781538341070 (library bound) | ISBN 9781538341094 (6 pack)
Subjects: LCSH: Alamo (San Antonio, Tex.)–Juvenile literature. | Alamo (San Antonio, Tex.)–Siege, 1836–Juvenile literature. | Texas–History–To 1846–Juvenile literature. | San Antonio (Tex.)–Buildings, structures, etc.--Juvenile literature.
Classification: LCC F390.H53 2019 | DDC 976.4'351–dc23

Manufactured in the United States of America

CPSIA Compliance Information: Batch #CS18PK: For Further Information contact Rosen Publishing, New York, New York at 1-800-237-9932

CONTENTS

REMEMBERING HISTORY

The phrase "Remember the Alamo!" dates back to 1836 when settlers and Mexican forces fought the Battle of the Alamo. The battle and the **siege** that led up to it were key events in the Texas **Revolution**.

Settlers in Texas—which belonged to Mexico at the time—wanted to earn their **independence**. A group of Texans captured San Antonio, where the Alamo, a former **mission** and fort, was located. They made their stand in the Alamo although they were badly outnumbered. Mexican forces killed most of them when those forces stormed the Alamo early on the morning of March 6, 1836. Texas forces later cried "Remember the Alamo!" during the final battle of the war. Today, the Alamo is a popular tourist stop where visitors can relive the Battle of the Alamo.

TEXAN SETTLERS—MOST OF WHOM CAME FROM THE UNITED STATES—AND MEXICAN FORCES FOUGHT AGAINST EACH OTHER IN THE TEXAS REVOLUTION.

Sources from the Past

This painting—*Fall of the Alamo* (1904)—shows the chaos of the Battle of the Alamo. In the center, Davy Crockett is using his rifle as a club. The artist, Robert Jenkins Onderdonk, wasn't present for the battle. Is this painting a primary source? Do you think it's a fair representation of the battle? Why or why not?

The painting isn't a primary source because it was created nearly 70 years after the Battle of the Alamo. The artist relied on stories about the battle to bring it to life.

THE SPANISH ARRIVE

Long before the Alamo and before the Spanish arrived in the area now known as Mexico and Texas, the area was home to a mix of Native American groups known as the Coahuiltecans. They were hunter-gatherers who lived in small family bands. The bands moved around with the seasons to find food. Bands sometimes came together to trade or to make use of seasonal food resources.

The first European to reach the area was the Spanish captain Alonso Álvarez de Pineda in 1519. Nine years later, a shipwrecked Spaniard named Álvar Núñez Cabeza de Vaca explored the region. He later wrote about the land and the Native American groups he had encountered. For the next century and a half, European explorers paid little attention to the area.

TODAY, CABEZA DE VACA'S ACCOUNT, TITLED *LA RELACIÓN (THE ACCOUNT)*, IS ONE OF THE MOST IMPORTANT PRIMARY SOURCES FOR INFORMATION ABOUT THE NATIVE PEOPLES OF TEXAS.

Capitulo primero: en q̃ cuenta quãdo partio el armada, y los officiales y gẽte que en ella yua.

A Diez y siete dias del mes d̃ Junio de mil y quinientos y veynte y siete partio del puerto de sant Lucar de Barrameda, el gouernador Pamphilo de Naruaez, con poder y mandado de vuestra magestad para conquistar y gouernar las prouincias q̃ estan desde el rio delas palmas hasta el cabo dela florida: las quales son en tierra firme. Y la armada que lleuaua eran cinco nauios: enlos quales poco mas o menos yrian seyscientos hombres. Los officiales que lleuaua (porque dellos se ha de hazer mencion) eran estos q̃ aqui se nombrã: Cabeça d̃ vaca por thesorero y por alguazil mayor, Alonso enrriquez, cõtador, Alõso de solis por fator de vuestra magestad y por veedor, yua vn frayle de la orden de sant Francisco por comissario que se llamaua fray Juan suarez cõ otros quatro frayles dela misma orden: llegamos ala isla de sancto Domingo, dõde estuuimos casi quarenta y cinco dias proueyendo nos de algunas cosas necessarias, señaladamente de cauallos. Aqui nos faltaron de nuestra armada mas de ciento y quarenta hombres, que se quisieron quedar alli por los partidos y promessas que los dela tierra les hizieron. De alli partimos y llegamos a Sanctiago (que es puerto enla isla de Cuba) donde en algunos dias que estuuimos el gouernador se rehizo de gente/de armas/y de cauallos. Suscedio alli que vn gentil hombre que se llamaua Vasco porcalle vezino dela villa dela Trinidad (que es enla misma ysla, ofrescio de dar al gouernador ciertos bastimentos q̃ tenia enla Trinidad: que es cient leguas del dicho puerto de Sanctiago. El gouernador con toda la armada partio pa

A iij

THE SPANISH MISSIONS

Spain became interested in the area again once the French tried to establish a settlement on the Gulf of Mexico. Lead by René-Robert La Salle, the French colony lasted only five years, but it made the Spanish take action to protect their claim to the territory.

Starting in the 1680s, Spanish soldiers and Catholic **missionaries** established missions throughout what is now Texas and northeastern Mexico. The missions had three purposes: to **convert** the Native Americans to the Catholic faith, to spread Spanish civilization in the "New World," and to keep outsiders from settling in Spain's new territories.

Some Native Americans chose to keep their usual ways of life over life in missions. Others valued the protection and regular food supply that missions offered.

THIS MAP, CREATED BY LUIS ANTONIO MENCHACA IN 1764, SHOWS THE LOCATION OF THE ALAMO (UPPER LEFT) AND SURROUNDING AREAS. MENCHACA OWNED ONE OF THE OLDEST AND LARGEST LAND GRANTS IN TEXAS.

Sources from the Past

Maps can be very valuable when learning about the past. This primary source shows the area of Texas where the San Antonio mission can be found. What else can you learn from this map? Do you think it was easy or difficult for people to move from one place to another? What does the map tell you about the land?

MISSION SAN ANTONIO DE VALERO

The Alamo wasn't originally a fortress. It was a mission named San Antonio de Valero. In 1718, Spanish soldiers and missionaries set up the mission and a fort called San Fernando de Béxar. They built them along the San Antonio River, in the area now known as San Antonio, Texas. They starting building the mission's church in 1744 but it was never completed. The church eventually became the building many know today as the Alamo.

In 1749, a group of Apaches agreed to become Christians in exchange for Spanish protection against the Comanches. Other Apaches, however, continued to raid the missions. In 1793, control of the mission passed from the church to local authorities. In 1803, a group of Spanish soldiers from Mexico moved into the mission.

HISTORIANS BELIEVE THE SPANISH SOLDIERS NAMED THE BUILDING "THE ALAMO." THE SOLDIERS MAY HAVE NAMED IT AFTER THE MEXICAN VILLAGE THEY HAD COME FROM: EL ALAMO PARRAS. ALSO, COTTONWOOD TREES SURROUNDED THE MISSION, AND THE SPANISH WORD FOR COTTONWOOD IS *ÁLAMO*.

ANGLO SETTLERS ARRIVE

Leaders in Mexico grew angry about the way Spain was ruling them. In 1821, a revolution led by Agustín de Iturbide, an officer in the Spanish army, led to Mexico's independence. Iturbide made himself president and then emperor, but he was a bad leader.

The Mexican government signed peace **treaties** with local Apache Indians. However, Comanche Indians continued to attack settlers in Mexico. In 1820, Texas had only 4,000 Mexican settlers. They were unable to **defend** the vast empty spaces of Texas, and the Spanish government had been unable to persuade more Mexicans to settle there.

THIS PORTRAIT OF ITURBIDE WAS PAINTED IN 1822 AFTER HE MADE HIMSELF EMPEROR OF MEXICO. IS IT A PRIMARY SOURCE? WHY OR WHY NOT?

The Spanish government decided to allow settlers from the United States to come to Texas, hoping that these Anglo (white, non-Spanish) settlers would help protect Mexicans from Comanche attacks.

AUSTIN'S 300

In 1821, Missouri businessman Moses Austin got approval from Spanish officials to start a colony in Texas. He told the officials that the settlers would be Catholic and would follow Spanish laws. Austin died before he got to see his dream come true.

In January 1822, Moses's son Stephen and 300 Missouri families settled in southeastern Texas. However, by this time the Spanish no longer controlled Mexico. At first, the new Mexican government refused to recognize the Anglo settlers' right to set up a colony, but Austin convinced them to allow it.

Sources from the Past

This portrait of Stephen Austin was painted in 1833 while Austin was in Mexico City. Portraits were once very popular, and they are important primary sources. Little details about the subject can help you decide what they were like and how they wanted to be seen by others. What do you know about Austin by looking at this portrait?

TO ENSURE THE COLONY'S LANDS WERE DIVIDED ACCORDING TO MEXICAN LAW, THE AREA HAD TO BE MEASURED AND MAPPED. AUSTIN AND TWO OTHER MEN MADE MAPS OF THE REGION AROUND 1822.

Austin became the *empresario*, or **administrative** agent, for the colony. He was responsible for controlling **immigration** into the colony, setting up the legal system, and giving land to settlers. He was also responsible for representing the settlers' interests and concerns to the Mexican government.

TENSIONS RISE

Soon after Anglo settlers arrived in Texas, **tensions** grew between them and the Mexican government. Most settlers were Protestants and refused to become Catholics. The settlers also resisted speaking Spanish and obeying Mexican laws. Soon there were more Anglo settlers in Texas than Mexicans, and many people in Mexico grew alarmed.

THIS MURAL SHOWS STEPHEN AUSTIN MEETING WITH THE MEXICAN LAND COMMISSIONER TO GIVE LAND TO THE COLONISTS IN 1823.

In 1830, the Mexican congress made it illegal for more U.S. settlers to come into Texas. In 1832 and 1833, Anglo settlers gathered in the town of San Felipe de Austin to protest the Mexican government's unfair treatment. In 1833, Stephen Austin traveled to Mexico City to discuss the settlers' concerns with the Mexican government. The new president of Mexico, Antonio López de Santa Anna, had Austin imprisoned for more than a year.

THE ONLY KNOWN IMAGE OF THE ALAMO BEFORE THE 1836 BATTLE WAS CREATED BY ARTIST SÁNCHEZ NAVARRO. HOWEVER, THIS IS A COPY OF THAT DRAWING MADE BY JEAN-LOUIS BERLANDIER.

Sources from the Past

Berlandier's drawing is a copy of Navarro's original drawing. Does that make it a primary source? If not, is it still valuable to people studying the past? Why or why not?

EDGING CLOSER TO WAR

In 1835, Santa Anna sent several hundred soldiers to San Antonio to disarm Anglo Texans and arrest anyone who opposed him. An army of settlers led by Stephen Austin laid siege to the Mexican troops in San Antonio de Béxar—which was a newer name for the town where the Alamo was located. The Anglo settlers launched a fierce attack on December 5, 1835. After five days of fighting, the Mexican troops surrendered and moved south. About 100 Anglo settlers then occupied the Alamo.

While the Siege of Béxar was taking place, other Texans held a meeting known as the Consultation to discuss the situation. The Consultation became Texas's **provisional** government. Sam Houston was commander in chief of the Texas army. He had the **broadside** shown on the next page printed to find volunteers to fight for Texas independence.

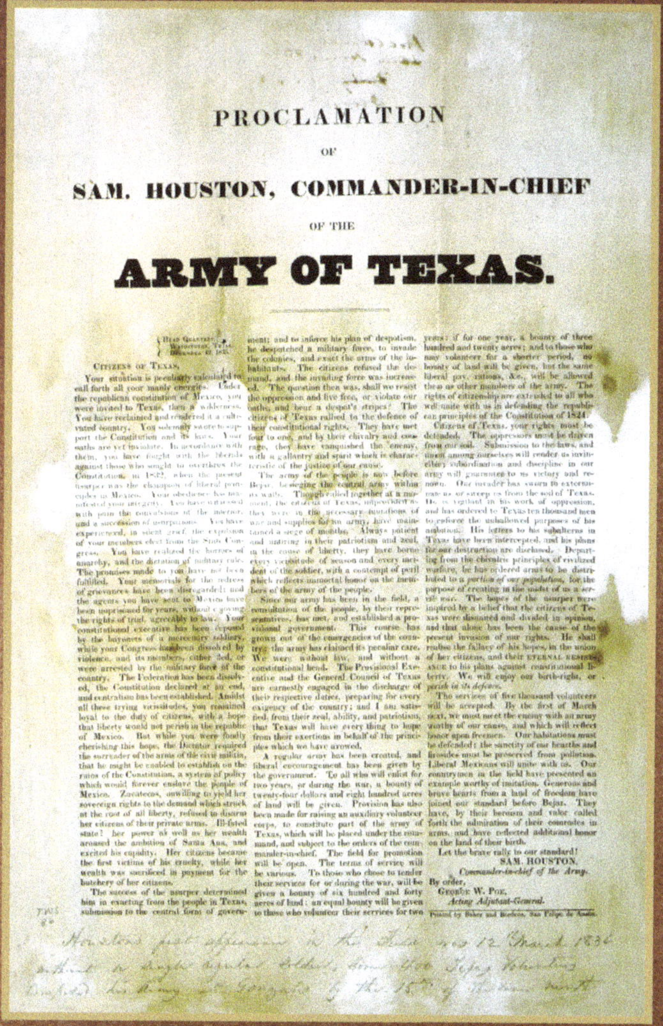

PROCLAMATION

OF

SAM. HOUSTON, COMMANDER-IN-CHIEF

OF THE

ARMY OF TEXAS.

SAM. HOUSTON,
Commander-in-chief of the Army.

By order,
GEORGE W. POE,
Acting Adjutant-General.

THIS IMAGE SHOWS HOUSTON'S ORIGINAL BROADSIDE. BELOW IT IS A TRANSCRIPTION OF THE TEXT IN THE BROADSIDE. A TRANSCRIPTION IS A WRITTEN REPRESENTATION OF SOMETHING. A TRANSCRIPTION CAN STILL BE CONSIDERED A PRIMARY SOURCE.

Sources from the Past

By the first of March next, we must meet the enemy with an army worthy of our cause, and which will reflect honor upon freemen. Our habitations must be defended; the sanctity of our hearths and firesides must be preserved from pollution... . Generous and brave hearts from a land of freedom have joined our standard before Bejar. They have, by their heroism and valor called forth the admiration of their comrades in arms, and have reflected additional honor on the land of their birth.

LEGENDARY FIGURES

Popular stories about the Alamo feature brave men who gave their lives to the cause for Texas independence. Later accounts turned them into larger-than-life heroes.

David "Davy" Crockett was one of the first to respond to the call for soldiers. Though Crockett had some success as a politician, he really gained national fame as a sharpshooter, hunter, and storyteller. Long before he arrived at the Alamo, David Crockett was a folk hero. Even during his life, a number of works—including a play and a book—turned Crockett into a legend.

Crockett met two other legends at the Alamo: James Bowie and William Barret Travis. Although legend surrounds these three figures, many choose to believe that they fought bravely at the Battle of the Alamo.

JAMES BOWIE

DAVY CROCKETT

ON JANUARY 9, 1863, CROCKETT WROTE THE FOLLOWING IN A LETTER: "I . . . HAVE ENROLLED MY NAME AS A VOLUNTEER [TO FIGHT FOR TEXAS'S INDEPENDENCE] AND WILL SET OUT FOR THE RIO GRAND IN A FEW DAYS WITH THE VOLUNTEERS FROM THE UNITED STATES . . . I AM IN HOPES OF MAKING A FORTUNE YET FOR MYSELF AND FAMILY."

THE SIEGE BEGINS

Volunteers slowly arrived at the Alamo, increasing the number of defenders to between 150 and 185. The majority of the defenders were Anglo, but there were also a few of Mexican descent. On February 23, 1836, Santa Anna arrived with around 1,800 soldiers and began the siege of the Alamo.

While Mexican forces waited outside the walls of the Alamo, Texas officials were preparing the Texas Declaration of Independence. This document mirrors the U.S. Declaration of Independence. It concludes by stating that the people of Texas had no choice but to declare Texas a free and independent **republic**. The declaration was approved and signed by the delegates on March 2, 1836. Soon after, they wrote the Texas Constitution and set up a provisional government.

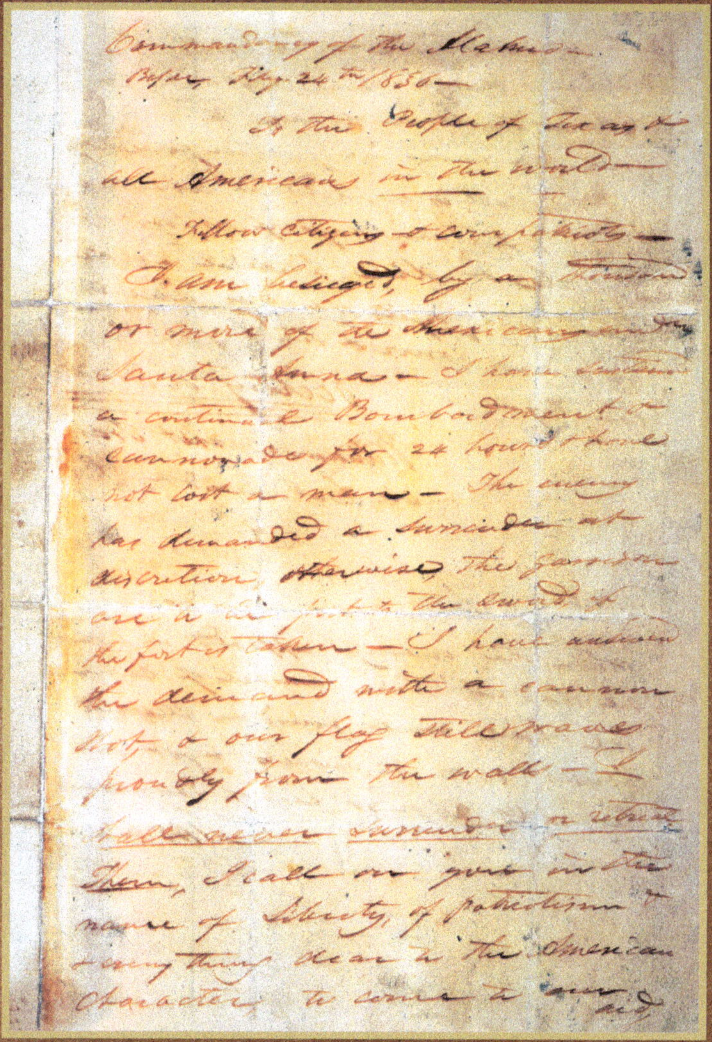
Commandancy of the Alamo—
Bejar, Feby. 24th 1836—
To the People of Texas & all Americans in the world—
Fellow citizens & compatriots—
I am besieged, by a thousand or more of the Mexicans under Santa Anna— I have sustained a continual Bombardment & cannonade for 24 hours & have not lost a man— The enemy has demanded a surrender at discretion, otherwise, the garrison are to be put to the sword, if the fort is taken— I have answered the demand with a cannon shot, & our flag still waves proudly from the walls— I shall never surrender or retreat. Then, I call on you in the name of Liberty, of patriotism & everything dear to the American character, to come to our aid

ON FEBRUARY 24, TRAVIS SENT A LETTER "TO THE PEOPLE OF TEXAS AND ALL AMERICANS IN THE WORLD," PLEADING FOR VOLUNTEERS. THE LETTER WAS PUBLISHED IN TWO NEWSPAPERS. HUNDREDS OF VOLUNTEERS RESPONDED TO TRAVIS'S PLEA, BUT NONE REACHED THE ALAMO IN TIME TO AID THE DEFENDERS.

Sources from the Past

This is a quote from Travis's letter:
"I shall never surrender or retreat. Then, I call on you in the name of Liberty, of patriotism, and everything dear to the American character, to come to our aid with all dispatch . . . . If this call is neglected, I am determined to sustain myself as long as possible and die like a soldier who never forgets what is due to his own honor and that of his country–Victory or Death."

BATTLE!

Santa Anna ordered his soldiers to attack the Alamo around 5 a.m. on March 6, 1836. The roughly 200 defenders inside the fort were no match for the almost 1,800 Mexican soldiers.

As the Mexican forces swarmed into the Alamo, Travis was one of the first defenders to die. The Texans locked themselves inside the buildings. Bowie, who had fallen ill on February 24, was killed on his cot. Crockett was killed as well, though there are different stories about how he died.

The battle lasted less than an hour and a half. Though all the defenders died, Santa Anna gave safe passage, a blanket, and two dollars to each woman, child, and slave inside the Alamo. This included Travis's slave, Joe.

THE SEIGE OF THE ALAMO IS SHOWN HERE IN THIS HAND-COLORED WOODCUT. LITTLE IS KNOWN ABOUT THE ORIGINAL ILLUSTRATION, BUT IT MAY HAVE BEEN CREATED IN THE 19TH CENTURY.

THE TEXAS REVOLUTION

Next, Santa Anna moved his army southeast toward Goliad. They caught up with a group of Texas soldiers and killed them. When word of this event reached Houston's men, some of them fled with their families. Houston took his remaining soldiers and followed Santa Anna's troops.

Houston's men caught up with the Mexican army on the San Jacinto River near Galveston Bay on April 20, 1836. On the afternoon of April 21, while the Mexican army was resting, Houston prepared to attack. With cries of "Remember the Alamo!" and "Remember Goliad!" the Texas army charged the sleeping Mexicans.

The bloody battle lasted only 18 minutes. When it was over, 630 Mexican soldiers had been killed and 730 had been taken prisoner. With the victory in the Battle of San Jacinto, Texans had won their independence.

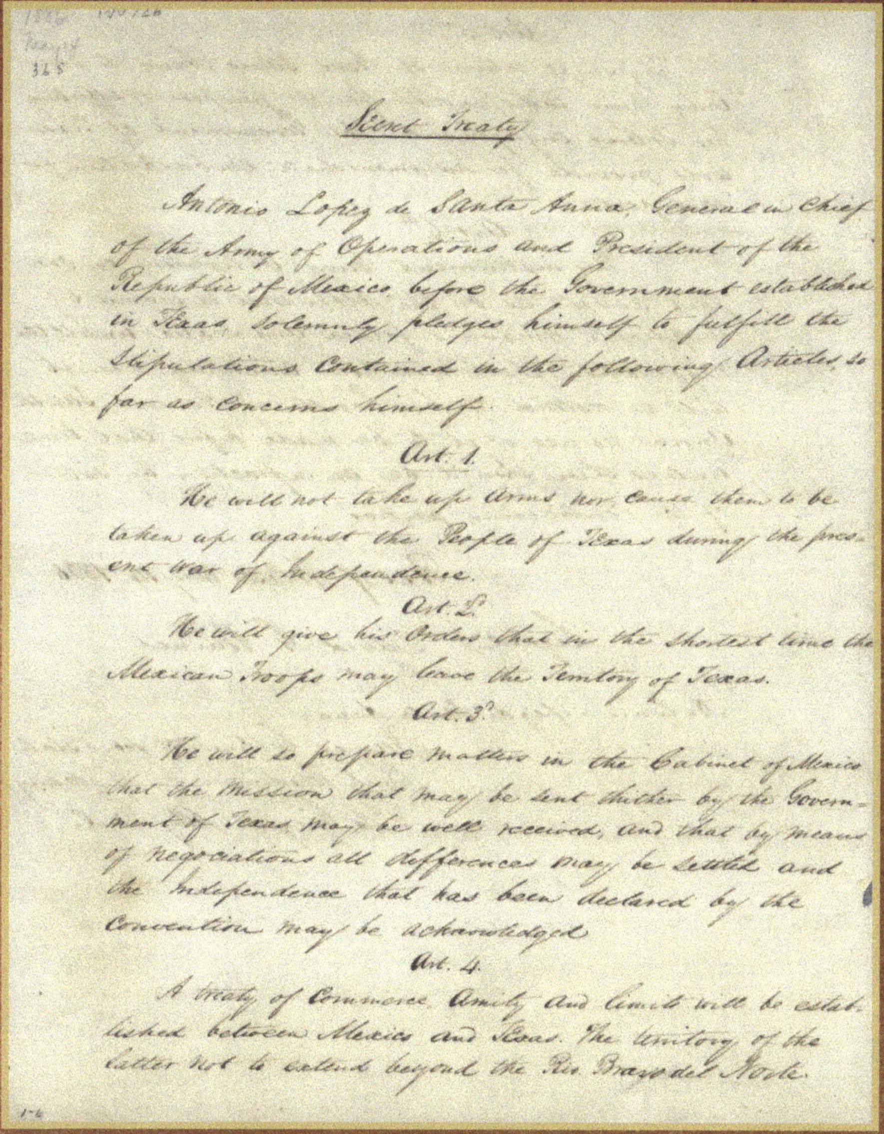

Secret Treaty

Antonio Lopez de Santa Anna, General in Chief of the Army of Operations and President of the Republic of Mexico before the Government established in Texas solemnly pledges himself to fulfill the Stipulations contained in the following Articles so far as concerns himself.

Art. 1.

He will not take up Arms nor cause them to be taken up against the People of Texas during the present War of Independence.

Art. 2.

He will give his Orders that in the Shortest time the Mexican Troops may leave the Territory of Texas.

Art. 3.

He will so prepare matters in the Cabinet of Mexico that the Mission that may be sent thither by the Government of Texas may be well received, and that by means of negociations all differences may be settled and the Independence that has been declared by the Convention may be acknowledged.

Art. 4.

A treaty of Commerce Amity and Limits will be established between Mexico and Texas. The territory of the latter not to extend beyond the Rio Bravo del Norte.

SHOWN HERE IS A TREATY SIGNED BY SANTA ANNA ON MAY 14, 1836. A PARTIAL TRANSCRIPTION IS SHOWN BELOW THE PRIMARY SOURCE.

Sources from the Past

Antonio López de Santa Anna, General in Chief of the Army of Operations and President of the Republic of Mexico, before the Government established in Texas, solemnly pledges himself to fulfill the stipulations contained in the following Articles, so far as concerns himself.

AFTER THE REVOLUTION

The Alamo was left in ruins. In 1841, the Republic of Texas returned control of the Alamo to the Catholic Church. Texas became part of the United States in 1846. The U.S. army began using it as a military supply yard in 1848. In 1850, the army started paying the church rent for the use of the building. Soon after, the army began to repair and update the church building.

In 1877, French businessman Honore Grenet opened a museum and general store at the Alamo. Grenet made grand updates to the buildings. For a time, he rented the church building and used it as a warehouse.

On April 23, 1883, the Texas legislature passed a bill authorizing the purchase of the Alamo and placing it under the care of the city of San Antonio.

THIS DRAWING OF THE ALAMO WAS MADE IN 1854. ALTHOUGH THE BUILDING WAS STILL IN RUINS, IT WAS ALREADY BECOMING A POPULAR TOURIST SPOT.

A LASTING SYMBOL OF STRENGTH

In 1903, the Alamo was nearly torn down to make room for a new hotel. San Antonio schoolteacher Adina De Zavala organized an effort to save the building. A wealthy woman named Clara Driscoll supplied the money to buy the Alamo. Driscoll specified that the property was "for the use and benefit of the Daughters of the Republic of Texas and is to be used by them for the purpose of making a park about the Alamo." The Daughters of the Republic of Texas no longer own the Alamo, but its members continue to make sure that the people who struggled to make Texas free are not forgotten.

The Alamo has become a symbol not only for the struggles of early Texans, but for the struggles of all U.S. citizens. By examining the primary sources in this book, we gain a deeper understanding of what those struggles really mean.

GLOSSARY

administrative: Having to do with running a government, company, school, or other organization.

broadside: A sheet of paper printed on one side only, forming one large page.

convert: To change from one thing into another.

defend: To fight back against an attack.

immigration: The act of coming to a country to settle there.

independence: The state of being free.

mission: A community established by a church for the purpose of spreading its faith.

missionary: Someone who travels to a new place to spread their faith.

provisional: Existing at the present, but likely to change later.

republic: A country governed by elected representatives and an elected leader.

revolution: The forceful overthrow of a government.

siege: The operations of an army around a place for the purpose of forcing its occupants to give up.

tension: A state in which people, groups, or countries disagree with and feel anger toward each other.

treaty: An official agreement made between two or more countries or groups.

INDEX

WEBSITES

Due to the changing nature of Internet links, PowerKids Press has developed an online list of websites related to the subject of this book. This site is updated regularly. Please use this link to access the list: www.powerkidslinks.com/eohs/alamo